The Retirement Tax Bon...

How to
Protect Your 401k
From Impending Tax Increases
And Create a Tax Free Retirement

Scott Newhouse, CFP®
Professor of Tax Planning, Cal State University -
Northridge

Table of Contents

A Word of Caution

First of all, congratulations for picking this book up!

Our country is facing some really interesting challenges, and one of the biggest is our government's financial situation. This book addresses those challenges and what it means for you and your money.

I need to caution you, though. I outline a number of strategies in this book. **Before you take action on any of them, please do yourself a favor and consult a certified financial planner and/or a tax professional.**

Limits of Liability and Disclaimer of Warranty:

The author shall not be liable for your misuse of this material. This book is strictly for educational purposes. Before implementing any of the strategies discussed in this book, please seek professional guidance.

About The Author

My name is Scott Newhouse and I work as a Certified Financial Planner™ in Thousand Oaks, CA. I run a Financial Planning firm called Forthright Finances (ForthrightFinances.com), where I help people have a secure and fulfilling retirement.

In addition to that, I am also an Adjunct Professor at Cal State University - Northridge, where I teach Tax and Estate Planning to college seniors majoring in Financial Planning.

In my free time, I love going to LA Clipper basketball games, watching the USC Trojans football team, reading about American history, and finding new hiking spots.

Free Bonus

In order for you to have the best understanding of the very important topics we will cover in this book, I have created a membership website.

The site is full of resources, worksheets, and videos that will help you have the retirement you deserve. The best part? It's completely free.

You can access it at www.retiretaxbomb.com

When you sign up, here's what you'll receive:
-Video breakdown of the strategies we discuss
-Worksheets and PDFs that you can customize to your specific situation. Specifically, you will get:
- -6 Steps To A Tax Free Retirement
- -Retirement Readiness Checklist
- -Retirement Income Worksheet
- -How To Avoid Losing $100,000 in Social Security Benefits
- -8 Steps to a Worry-Free Retirement
- -Calculating Your Tax Buckets
- -Access to all additional resources and links

To get these helpful resources, go to
www.retiretaxbomb.com

Chapter One: Lowest Taxes Of Our Lifetime?

Do you know about the history of taxation in the United States?

I'm not talking about historical moments like the Stamp Act, which kickstarted the Revolutionary War. I'm talking about the history of tax brackets in the U.S.

<u>Do you know what the highest tax bracket in this nation was?</u>

If you can avoid looking ahead, take a guess as to what the highest tax bracket was in our country's history.

Ready for it?

It is a whopping 94%! Yes, you read that right. In 1945, the highest income tax rate was 94%.

That rate has dropped throughout the last 7 decades.

In the 1960s, the highest tax rate decreased to 70%. And it remained at that level for the 1970s.

In 1980, the rate dropped even more, down to 50%.

And today, thanks to the tax cuts that President Trump signed into law in 2017, our highest marginal tax rate is 37%.

I am sure you have, but I have to ask: Have you noticed a trend here?

Over the last 7 decades, our country has continually lowered our tax rates. And the historically low tax rates we have today presents a tremendous opportunity for you and your retirement.

And that's exactly what this book is about - how our country's financial situation <u>will</u> affect your retirement.

This book is applicable to anyone who is concerned about their money, investments and retirement.

But it is especially written for the following people:

- You are anywhere from five to fifteen years away from retirement.
- You have worked hard for your entire career and now you want to make sure that you retire the right way and get what you have earned.
- You do not want to pay any unnecessary taxes.

And here is what you can expect to learn from this book.

- You will learn that the balances in your IRA and your 401K are not exactly what you think they will be.
- You will learn about the best strategies to protect your money from impending tax increases.
- You will learn how to create a tax free retirement.
- You will learn the right amounts to have in each type of financial account you have
- You will learn how the government is taxing you twice on your social security - and how to avoid that extra tax payment

What Stands In The Way Of A Great Retirement

We all dream of that day when we finally have the choice to never work again. When we can still work if we want, but work is optional, not a necessity.

It's something all of us are working towards, and for good reason. Maybe you want to spend more time with the grandkids, pick up that hobby that you never had enough time for, rediscover your passions, or do something completely different.

So how do you have that kind of retirement?

To answer that, I think it's most helpful to start with the main obstacles to a great retirement.

From my experience as a financial planner and working with retirees, here are a few obstacles I've seen people encounter along the way:

- A lack of proper planning (in terms of finances, lifestyle, or otherwise) for your retirement
- Market volatility and the uncertainty that comes with investing in the stock market
- The loss of purchasing power and the reduction of your dollar's capability
- The ever-present threat of inflation
- Taxes, taxes and taxes

Each of these issues can pose problems for you as a potential retiree.

For instance, let's say you have saved a lot of money for your retirement. You might (and should) be proud of this achievement. With a hefty amount of savings, you can feel like you're on top of the world.

But beware: Your retirement account balance may not be what you think it is.

If you're like most people, you have your retirement money in Traditional IRAs and Traditional 401Ks.

What does "traditional" mean? It means that the government hasn't taken its share of that money yet (ie, you haven't paid taxes on it yet).

In other words: the government owns a percentage of that money, and has the legal right to take it in the future.

Beyond that, the government also has the ability to increase the percentage of money that it owns from those accounts whenever it wants!

You might think I'm crazy to be talking about higher tax rates, especially when I just told you about how tax rates have been going lower and lower for decades.

But in the next two chapters, I'm going to tell you the financial challenges facing our country that make increasing tax rates all but a certainty.

Chapter 1 Key Takeaways:

- Tax rates are at historic lows - this presents a massive opportunity for you and your retirement
- There are a number of obstacles to a great retirement - you need to address all of them
- The savings in your IRAs and 401Ks are not always what they seem to be - the government owns a percentage of that money

- The government can increase that amount they own whenever they want (in the form of higher taxes)
- Just because taxes are low today doesn't mean they will be low forever

Free Resources:
- 8 Steps to a Worry-Free Retirement

To get these helpful resources, go to:

www.retiretaxbomb.com

Chapter Two: 5 Financial Threats Facing Our Country

Think back to those Saturday mornings you spent watching the classic *Looney Tunes* cartoons with your kids.

Remember the ones that focused on the ongoing battle between the Roadrunner versus Wile E. Coyote?

Wile E. Coyote, to put it kindly, did not do too well in this matchup. He simply couldn't avoid whatever trick the Roadrunner came up with.

Whether it was anvils dropping from the sky, tunnels that led to nowhere, or an oncoming train on railroad tracks, it seemed like Wile E. Coyote was always getting hit. He never avoided any threat and the Roadrunner was always one step ahead of him.

That last example I mentioned is one that I think relates well to us today: Wile E. Coyote is sitting on the train tracks, and he sees the train coming right at him.

If you want a laugh, take a minute to check it out on Youtube. If you search "Wile E Coyote Freight Train" that should get you there.

When the train is coming at Wlie E. Coyote, he has two choices: He can get the heck out of the way, or he can stay put and do nothing.

What does he do? He pulls the blinds for the window down, as if that will make the problem go away. And then he stays put, on the train tracks, and doesn't move a muscle. Which inevitably leads him to being hit by the train.

I think we've all been faced with situations like this before. Where we know that there is a problem ahead, and we can either do something about it, or we can sit back, do nothing and pretend the problem doesn't exist.

Are you guilty of that? I know I am.

I think the fiscal situation our country faces creates a metaphorical "tax train" that is coming towards us in the form of much higher taxes.

And these higher taxes represent something that could completely blow up your retirement plan.

Which is why I warn every potential retiree I talk to about what I call a Retirement Tax Bomb.

And I need to ask you: Do you want to avoid the retirement tax bomb or do you want to pretend it isn't a problem, like Wile E. Coyote?

I know some of you might think that I'm going overboard with my concern. So I want to explain just what is so perilous about our country's finances.

To start, a quick reminder:

- Seventy years ago, tax rates on personal income were really high - up to 94%!
- After the Tax Cuts and Jobs Act of 2017, this rate has decreased exponentially. Now, the highest rate is 37%.
- However, at the end of 2025, these tax cuts are going to expire - and we will go back to the higher, pre-2017 tax rates
- This means that if Congress does nothing (sound familiar?) then in six years (as of Jan 2020), tax rates *will* rise.

So tax rates are set to go up in the future.

But could they rise even higher after that? Will the tax rates we have now be all-time historical low?

I think a good case could be made that the answer to both of those questions is "Yes!"

There are five major reasons to be worried about much higher taxes coming in the near future.

Reason One: Not Enough Workers

In 1945, we had about 42 workers who were able to support 1 social security recipient (by paying into payroll taxes). Yet the number of workers has fallen dramatically over the last 7 decades.

As of 2010, the number of workers per social security recipient has dropped to just under 3 workers.

Think about that. 42/1 in 1945 and only 3/1 in 2010.

The problem with this lack of workers is that we depend on them to fund many of our social programs, including social security. <u>And if the government can't get the money to fund social security from these workers, then they're going to search for it in other areas.</u>

Reason Two: Too Many Retirees

As the population continues to grow over time, so too does the number of people who retire every day. In 1980, the number of people reaching the age of 65 daily was just over 5,000.

That number held true up until about 2000 when massive spikes in the number of retirees began to occur. Today, there are 10,000 people turning 65 every day in the U.S.

According to Census projections, this tally will rise to 12,000 per day.

So we are stuck in a really tough spot: We have less workers, and more retirees than ever before. Which puts an enormous strain on our country's ability to fund many of our social programs.

Reason Three: Steady Increase In Mandatory Spending (Social Security, Medicare, Medicaid)

When we look at the government's budget, it's mainly divided into three categories.

First is discretionary spending, which Congress can adjust on a year to year basis.

Second is net interest. This is essentially what we are paying in interest payments for all the money we have borrowed.

Third is mandatory spending. Mandatory spending is money that the federal government has promised, by law, to go to certain programs. The most common programs in mandatory spending are Social Security, Medicare, and Medicaid.

Our government budgets have undergone a massive shift over the past fifty years.

In 1968 (back when we had many more workers per retiree) the percentage allocated to mandatory spending in the federal budget was just 28%.

On the other end of the spectrum, the rate of discretionary spending was at a whopping 66%. This simply meant that the government could decide how it wanted to spend 66% of its revenues on a year to year basis.

In other words, how they spent this money was up for grabs. The other 28% (the mandatory spending) had to be spent on Social Security, Medicare, and Medicaid.

Over time, though, these numbers began to shift. Now, mandatory spending takes up 61% of our country's budget, and discretionary spending accounts for just 31% of the budget.

And over the course of the next decade, we can expect this to get even worse, as mandatory spending will reach 64% and discretionary spending will only be 23%.

What is causing this mandatory spending?

There are three primary examples of automatic expenditures that have consumed a larger share of the budget than in years past.
- Social Security, a retirement benefits program

- Medicare, a health insurance program for everyone over the age of 65.
- Medicaid, a health insurance program for low income individuals and families.

Why does this increase in mandatory spending matter?

It means that our politicians, who love to spend money, will have less money to use for their own purposes. Which, in my mind, won't be something they will be happy about.

At some point, they will look for additional avenues to find money to spend that won't have to go to the mandatory spending programs.

Where do you think they get that money from.....

Reason Four: Trust Fund Depletion

Both Social Security and Medicare are currently paid for by a combination of two sources: Payroll taxes (paid by workers), and Trust Funds.

Social Security and Medicare have their own separate Trust Fund that they use to pay for their programs, in addition to what they receive from payroll taxes.

Right now, we depend on payroll taxes to pay for most of these programs. And we use the trust funds to pay for the remaining balance.

But we have a huge problem: Since we've been using the money in the trust fund for many years, we're depleting the amount in each fund. <u>And soon - within the next 10-15 years, both trust funds will be completely depleted.</u>

This is a huge problem - as I just mentioned, payroll taxes can't currently fund both programs. And it's only going to get worse, since we don't have enough workers paying into the system.

By the time that each trust fund runs out, payroll taxes will only account for 75% of Social Security benefits and 90% of Medicare benefits.

So what will the government do to address this problem? They have two main options, in my mind:

One, they can drastically cut benefits.

Two, they can drastically increase taxes.

I think the second is far more likely, and I'll explain why in just a few pages.

The main thing you need to ask yourself right now is:

<u>Where will our government get the money to make up the difference between the promised benefits and the expected tax shortfall to pay for those benefits?</u>

Reason Five: Rapidly Increasing Debts, Deficits, and Interest Rates

It's hard to fully appreciate how much our country's debt, our deficits, and our interest payments have grown over the past few decades.

In 2000, our national debt was around $5.5 trillion. Today (January 2020), it is just over $23 trillion. And this rapid growth isn't expected to slow down anytime soon!

Next is our federal deficits. In other words, does our government spend more money than it takes in?

In the last 3 decades, there have only been 4 years where the government brought in more money than it spent. Which means Congress is spending too much virtually every year.

Lastly, we are paying a lot of money on our debt payments. Our country is paying over $750 billion in *interest payments* to pay down the debt that we have (including a sizeable amount owed to China, by the way).

What do we make of all of this? I'm sure there's a lot that could be said, but let me offer just a few thoughts.

1. Our government loves to spend money, and has little to no interest in cutting what it spends.

2. Our government focuses on the here and now, and is less inclined to think through the consequences of their actions, especially when those consequences are delayed for 10 plus years.

Why is that? I hate to be cynical, but they may no longer be in political office at that point, so as long as it doesn't affect their re-election chances, they may not care too much.

So we've just gone through 5 major financial threats facing our country.

As I've said before, the question we all have to ask ourselves is: What will the government do about them?

The two broad options are to cut benefits, and increase taxes.

In the next chapter, I'll detail why I think higher taxes are much more likely than cutting benefits.

Key Takeaways:

- In 2026, tax rates will increase. It is set into law and will happen as long as Congress does nothing.
- We simply don't have enough workers paying taxes to support the number of retirees who receive Social Security/Medicare benefits.
- 10,000 people turn 65 years old daily, making them eligible for benefits they have earned.
- Our government is forced to spend a higher and higher percentage of its budget on mandatory spending (like Social Security and Medicare), lessening how much it can allocate to other programs and services.
- The Social Security and Medicare Trust Funds will be depleted within the next 10-15 years, at which point those programs will only rely on payroll taxes. But payroll taxes won't be enough to cover all of the benefits people are entitled to receive.
- The national debt, deficits and interest payments are growing at a rapid pace, with little concern from politicians about the long term consequences.

Free Resources:
- Retirement Readiness Checklist

Get this free resource at: www.retiretaxbomb.com

Chapter Three: Why Taxes Must Rise

When it comes to Social Security and Medicare, there have been a number of potential solutions. The five most common ones are:

- Push back the age for full benefits
- Lower the inflation increases (for Social Security)
- Tax Social Security benefits (even more)
- Decrease benefit amounts/coverages
- Raise the contribution amounts (ie, taxes) of working Americans

These solutions might seem like common sense ideas that rational people can compromise, negotiate and eventually agree on. Right?

Hah! Unfortunately, as I'm sure you're aware, our political system doesn't exactly work like that.

For instance, let's look at Paul Ryan, a former Congressman from Wisconsin. Ryan is known as a fiscal conservative, who is deeply concerned about the debt, deficits, and the growing benefits of Social Security, Medicare, and our country's future inability to fund them.

So in 2011 he proposed a budget that would make major changes to the system in an effort to stabilize and sustain Social Security and Medicare. In particular, he suggested pushing back the age you are entitled to benefits, as well as limiting the costs of these programs.

It was a very detailed plan, which we don't have the time to explore here. But the essence of it is that it did represent a cut in some benefits for these programs.

So what happened next? Was there a good faith argument about the merits of his proposed budget?

Nope! Not even close.

Instead of doing that, his opponents made an advertisement showing him push an elderly lady off of a cliff. Yes, you read that correctly.

Paul Ryan's proposed changes to Social Security and Medicare were portrayed as throwing your sweet ole grandma off to her untimely death.

Needless to say, Paul's changes were not adopted, and nothing in terms of these programs or our country's fiscal crisis was changed.

What's the point of this story?

That anyone who wants to change (or more specifically, cut) Social Security or Medicare benefits is in for a rude awakening.

Politicians want to get re-elected, and they know that one of the largest, most vocal, and most likely to vote voting blocs are people over the age of 50. And those people don't want to see their Social Security or Medicare benefits lowered.

Which is why I've said throughout this book that if our country is going to make changes to Social Security or Medicare, tax increases are far more likely than benefit cuts.

But don't just take my word.

Meet David Walker

David Walker was the head of the General Accounting Office during the administration of President George W. Bush. He is not a partisan who is focused on getting one political party in power. He's focused on the math and this country's financial future, and that's why I think his advice is worth listening to.

Here's what he thinks about our current situation:

- According to him, tax increases are inevitable. However, the quicker we make changes, the smaller the changes we would need to make.
- Conversely, the longer we wait, the bigger the changes we will have to make.

- Why must we make these changes? According to him, one four letter word is the answer: Math. We mathematically cannot sustain what we are doing.
- Between a ballooning debt and growing deficits, coupled with future obligations in mandatory spending, our historically low tax rates are in danger.
- **Because of this confluence of circumstances, Walker thinks tax rates will need to double.**

This point brings us back to the example I shared earlier about Wile E. Coyote sitting on the train tracks watching the train come right at him. In the same way that Wile E. Coyote could see the train coming at him, we can very clearly see tax increases headed straight at us.

And this poses an essential question: Should we also pull the curtain down and pretend there isn't a problem? Or should we take action now to get off the train tracks and avoid dramatically higher tax rates?

The good news of this situation is that a historic opportunity has been presented to us…. We have the ability to avoid these higher tax rates and instead pay taxes at historically low rates.

We are enjoying these low tax rates thanks to the Tax Cuts and Jobs Act of 2017.

Signed into law in December 2017, it lowered individual tax rates from 2018 through 2025. Which means that as of me writing this (January 2020), we will only have 6 tax years left of these lower rates.

And once we get to January 1, 2026, tax rates will increase.

But lowering the tax rate wasn't the only boon for this law. It also expanded the tax brackets, which allowed individuals to earn even more money at lower rates.

For your reference, here are the 2019 tax brackets for different filing status:

Tax rate	Single	Married, filing jointly	Married, filing separately	Head of household
10%	$0 to $9,700	$0 to $19,400	$0 to $9,700	$0 to $13,850
12%	$9,701 to $39,475	$19,401 to $78,950	$9,701 to $39,475	$13,851 to $52,850
22%	$39,476 to $84,200	$78,951 to $168,400	$39,476 to $84,200	$52,861 to $84,200
24%	$84,201 to $160,725	$168,401 to $321,450	$84,201 to $160,725	$84,201 to $160,700
32%	$160,726 to $204,100	$321,451 to $408,200	$160,726 to $204,100	$160,701 to $204,100
35%	$204,101 to $510,300	$408,201 to $612,350	$204,101 to $306,175	$204,101 to $510,300
37%	$510,301 or more	$612,351 or more	$306,176 or more	$510,301 or more

I do need to warn you, though. Having this knowledge will only take you so far.

To get the benefits of the strategies I will talk about in this book, you have to commit to taking action. The sooner you take action, the better, for you and your retirement.

Here are three key reasons why you need to act now or risk subjecting yourself to gigantic tax increases.

1. Right now, we are experiencing historically low tax rates.
    a. Tax rates have dropped from 94% all the way down to 37%.
2. Tax rates are set to increase in six years.
    a. It may seem like six years is a long time away, but every year you don't take action is another year of not taking advantage of low tax rates.
3. Taxes are going to rise even higher.
    a. In addition to tax increases in 2026, there is a very strong possibility of taxes going even higher after that. Between the national debt, interest rates, deficits, Social Security, and Medicare, there is too much to pay for at our current tax rates.

I know that so far, this probably hasn't been the most uplifting message.

But I do have good news for you: We know exactly when tax rates are set to increase.

You see, most problems do not have an identifiable. They just happen, and sometimes suddenly.

We don't have to worry about that, as we know exactly when taxes will increase.

And the only question left for us is: Do we stay on the train tracks as the Retirement Tax Bomb comes straight at us? Or do we act now to get out of the way?

Key Takeaways:

- It is extremely unlikely that Congress will ever have the stomach to cut benefits. There are too many people (and political parties) against that
- The most likely solution for Congress will be to raise taxes
- Like it or not, taxes will increase on January 1, 2026.
- Because of the number of financial issues facing this country, taxes are likely to rise dramatically higher in the future (above the 2026 rates).

- We have two choices, but only one makes sense. We can ignore the problem, or we can take action today to avoid this Retirement Tax Bomb.

Free Resources:
- How To Avoid Losing $100,000 in Social Security Benefits

Get this free resource at: www.retiretaxbomb.com

Chapter Four: How The Retirement Tax Bomb Can Ruin Your Retirement

So far, we've talked a lot about the issues facing our country, and some of the potential solutions to those problems. But what we still need to explore is how all of this can affect you.

To help us do that, let's take a look at a couple who have begun to think about retirement. You might recognize them from one of my favorite shows growing up, I Love Lucy.

Meet Lucy and Ricky!

- Lucy and Ricky are both 55 years old. They want to retire at the age of sixty-five. With retirement only 10 years away, they have begun to think about this transition.
- Throughout their careers, Lucy and Ricky did very well for themselves.
- Recently, the pair moved to Las Vegas. Of course, in Nevada, there is no state income tax.
- Throughout their working careers, Lucy and Ricky lived in an expensive apartment. Las Vegas is quite a change of pace for them.
- For the past thirty years, Ricky has worked hard and will receive Social Security.
- Lucy worked sporadically at odd jobs, so her Social Security benefit won't be much. That's

okay though, as she'll be able to take Spousal Social Security Benefits.

It seems like Lucy and Ricky might be in pretty good shape as they approach retirement. But what does their financial picture currently look like? Let's examine it.

- After living in an apartment for their entire lives, Lucy and Ricky decided to finally pay for a house. It was not a cheap purchase either! The house is worth $500,000.
- In Ricky's Traditional 401(k), there is currently $300,00 saved up. Not bad!
- In Ricky's Traditional IRA, there is currently $200,000.
- Additionally, Ricky and Lucy have $100,000 in mutual funds in a taxable account
- On top of it all, they have no debt.
- Ricky's Social Security benefits are currently expected to clock in at a rate of $36,000 per year.
- Ricky and Lucy want to retire on $6,000 per month, or $72,000 per year.
- In total, this brings the net worth of Lucy and Ricky to $1,100,000.

Ricky and Lucy have undoubtedly done well for themselves. And retirement probably seems like a breeze, right?

[handwritten margin notes: "not enough equity & huge mort", "return", "taxes due", "taxes due", "Capital Gains taxes due", "taxes due"]

Well, not exactly. You see, Ricky and Lucy have put themselves in a very dangerous position. They are highly susceptible to taxes, and tax increases, blowing up their retirement plan.

And they, like all of us, have two choices, but only one makes sense.

Do they ignore the impending tax increases and take their chances that the federal government won't increase taxes too much?

Or do they take action now to lock in historically low tax rates so that tax increases in the future won't blow up their retirement?

Where Ricky and Lucy Went Wrong

Let's assume, using the information we listed out above, that Ricky and Lucky chose to ignore the impending tax increases our country faces.

What will their lives look like at 65? And what does their life look like as a result of not locking in lower tax rates?

Here are a few of the problems that Lucy and Ricky will encounter because they closed their eyes to the retirement tax bomb coming our way:

- Let's assume that their retirement accounts grew from $500K up to $1 million. They sadly don't actually own that $1 million. Remember, since they have never paid taxes on this money, the IRS actually has partial ownership of this lump sum. So the government owns 20-30% of that amount!
- Further, they are extremely vulnerable to tax increases. As tax rates rise in the coming years, they are slated to own even less of their retirement accounts.
- Even worse, they will have no option but to pay those higher taxes, since they didn't plan ahead for this possibility. In other words, because of their inaction, they limited their options in retirement.
- Almost all of their Social Security will be subject to taxation. Specifically, 85% of their Social Security will be taxed. This is because their income is too high in retirement, which the IRS punishes people for by taxing their Social Security.
- To add insult to injury, this means that they will pay taxes on Social Security TWICE. First, they paid payroll taxes when they were working. And now, they are paying taxes on their benefits in retirement. Ouch.
- All of these unexpected (to them) tax payments mean that they need to distribute more and more money out of their investment portfolios just to pay their tax bill every April 15.

- Additionally, they have far too much money in taxable accounts, which increases their income and forces them to pay even more in taxes.
- Lastly, Ricky and Lucy do not have any tax-free income streams. Which limits their options, and frankly, their odds to have a secure, stress free retirement.

Adjusted taxable income and tax bracket

✳ Tax bracket ◉ Key tax components

● Adjusted taxable income w/ conversion   ● Adjusted taxable income w/o conversion

Ricky and Lucy's taxable income throughout retirement.

Note: In the chart above, it is showing a projection of Ricky and Lucy's taxable income in retirement, which will leave them paying a ton in taxes. I ran this scenario in my financial planning software, which you have access to when you sign up for my free bonus at www.retiretaxbomb.com

As we saw in this chapter, Ricky and Lucy are getting taxed in every direction. Their retirement accounts, their taxable accounts, and even their Social Security benefits are being taxed.

But what's especially sad about their situation is that all of this could have been avoided. They do not have to have this tax bomb in their retirement, and neither do you.

And that's what we're going to talk about in the next chapter: <u>The Six Steps To A Tax Free Retirement.</u>

Key Takeaways:

- Ricky and Lucy have saved a decent amount of money, but they own the government a percentage of it
- Because they didn't plan ahead, they will be subject to much higher taxes in the future
- They will have to pay taxes on their retirement accounts, their taxable accounts, and their social security accounts
- The amount of taxes they have to pay will increase what they need to withdraw from their investment accounts (to pay for higher taxes), thereby lowering their odds of a stress-free and secure retirement
- None of this was necessary – careful planning could have dramatically lowered – or eliminated – their taxes in retirement
- There are six key steps to a tax free retirement – detailed in the next chapter

Free Resources:

- <u>Retirement Income Worksheet</u>: Calculate your retirement income so you know exactly what to expect when you retire.

Get this free resource at: www.retiretaxbomb.com

Chapter Five: Six Important Steps to Tax Free Retirement

As we saw with Ricky and Lucy, we know what the biggest risk is: Doing Nothing.

Following that path will lead to higher taxes, less flexibility, less security, and more stress.

So what should we do instead?

Follow the six steps to a tax free retirement.

But before we get started with these steps, I need to remind you:

This book is for educational purposes. To make sure that one, or all, of these strategies are right for you, in your specific situation, I highly recommend you consult with a financial professional. It's well worth it to hire a professional to make sure you are doing everything correctly.

Lastly, you cannot forget about state and local taxes. Your taxes will vary depending on where you live. To keep things simple in this illustration, we are assuming Ricky and Lucy live in Nevada, where there is no state income tax.

With all that said, let's get started on the six steps to avoid the retirement tax bomb and create a tax free retirement.

Step One To A Tax Free Retirement:
Calculate Your Tax Buckets

Have you heard of the term tax buckets before? It's a simple concept. As you know, there are different types of financial accounts that are taxed in different ways.

Some accounts are taxable every year, like your checking, savings and non-retirement investment accounts.

Other accounts are tax deferred, like your Traditional 401K and Traditional IRA. Tax deferred simply means you don't have to pay taxes on that money when you earn it, but delay paying those taxes to when you distribute that money in the future.

And finally, there are tax-free accounts. This means that no more taxes are due for money in these accounts, so you are free to withdraw money from them without having to worry about taxes. The most common example of this is a Roth account (it can either be a Roth IRA or Roth 401K).

As you head into retirement, we want to make sure you have the right amount of money in the right accounts. This strategy is essential if you want to minimize - or even eliminate - your taxes in retirement.

Taxable: I recommend keeping six months to one year of living expenses in a savings account. This is strictly as an emergency fund, in case one-time expenses pop up and you need cash quickly.

However, you don't want too much in your taxable bucket!

That's especially true if it's generating income (like capital gains or dividends).

Why? Because that will push up your taxable income, which will obviously increase your taxes owed. But it could also make your Social Security subject to taxation! We'll dive more into this in just a little bit.

Tax Deferred: Again, tax deferred is the same thing as your Traditional IRA or Traditional 401K. In my experience, this is where most people have most of their retirement assets.

The amount that you want in the tax deferred bucket is a little tricky. Try to stick with me here though, as this tax bucket amount is really important.

You want to have a decent amount of your retirement money in the tax deferred bucket, but you don't want to have all of your retirement assets in here either.

Why? Because if you have too much, you will be subject to higher income taxes, which will be especially harmful when tax rates rise in 2026. It'll be even worse for you if taxes rise dramatically even more (as I think they will). And the kicker, as I've said before, is if your income is too high, then almost all of your Social Security benefits will be taxed. Yikes!

But you also don't want too little in the tax deferred bucket. The reason for that is because the government allows you to not pay taxes on a certain amount of income every year. This is known as the standard or itemized deduction. It's essentially a way for us taxpayers to reduce our taxable income by a certain amount.

12,550 for single

Most people in retirement will be using the standard deduction, which for a married couple over 65, is $27,000 (as of 2019).

That means that you will not have to pay taxes on the first $27,000 of income that you have in retirement.

As you may know, when you turn 70.5, you will have to take something called a Required Minimum Distribution (RMD) out of your tax deferred accounts and pay taxes on it. The IRS mandates this because

$$X \cdot 3.65\% = 12,550 \qquad X =$$

$$\frac{}{3.65} \qquad \frac{}{3.65}$$

you haven't paid taxes on this money yet, and they want that revenue.

As of 2019, the IRS mandates that you withdraw 3.65% of your tax deferred accounts in that first year of RMDs.

Are you still with me? I hope so! I'm about to put it all together right now.

Your strategy should be: Have enough in your tax deferred accounts so that your RMD amount is roughly equal to your standard deduction.

In other words…. Let's say you have $740,000 in Traditional 401K and Traditional IRAs. At age 70.5, the government will make you take out 3.65%.

The calculation for how much you have to take out is quite simple:

$740,000 X 3.65% = $27,010.

Notice anything about the $27,010 that you have to take out? That's right, it's basically equal to your standard deduction amount! (Please excuse me for the extra $10, trying to keep the numbers simple :)

Why is this strategy so important? Because if you take out $27,000 from your tax deferred accounts,

you can offset that income with your standard
deduction of $27,000.

**Which means that the income you took from your
tax deferred accounts is entirely tax free!**

Tax-Free: The amount you should have in your tax
free accounts is much simpler to explain, thankfully!

Any amount that exceeds the limits set in the first two
categories should be redirected to tax-free accounts.

I do need to warn you, though. There's a temptation
to put everything in the tax-free buckets. I would
advise against that. Why? Because then you are
essentially giving up the standard deduction that
offsets your income in retirement.

Instead, I encourage you to have the right amounts in
each type of these three account types.

*Author's note: This tax bucket strategy is really
important, but can frankly be a little confusing,
especially trying to explain it in book format. If you
want to make sure you understand everything
properly, I'm happy to set up quick call with you and
answer any questions. Email
Scott@ForthrightFinances.com and we will set up a
time to talk.*

Step Two To A Tax Free Retirement:
Know Your Provisional Income and Marginal Tax Rate

Tax Filing Status	Provisional Income	Social Security Taxation
Single or head of household	Less than $25,000	0%
	$25,000 - $34,000	Up to 50%
	More than $34,000	Up to 85%
Joint filers	Less than $32,000	0%
	$32,000 - $44,000	Up to 50%
	More than $44,000	Up to 85%

(Provisional Income For 2019)

There are two tax terms that are essential to know as you head into retirement: Your provisional income and your marginal tax rate.

What is provisional income? It is a measure of income that the IRS uses to calculate how much Social Security benefits are taxed.

How do you calculate provisional income? You add up your gross income, as well as your tax free interest (like Municipal bonds), along with 50% of your Social Security benefits.

Once you have calculated your provisional income, then you can find out how much (if any) of your Social Security benefits will be taxed.

Ideally, your provisional income will be low enough so that you will not have to pay taxes on your Social Security benefits.

Next, we need to determine your marginal tax rate. Your marginal tax rate is the tax rate incurred on each dollar of additional income.

In other words, what is the highest tax rate you pay on your last dollar of income? That's your marginal tax rate.

RATE	SINGLE FILERS	MARRIED FILERS
10%	$0 – $9,700	$0 – $19,400
12%	$9,701 – $39,475	$19,401 – $78,950
22%	$39,476 – $84,200	$78,951 – $168,400
24%	$84,201 – $160,725	$168,401 – $321,450
32%	$160,726 – $204,100	$321,451 – $408,200
35%	$204,101 – $510,300	$408,201 – $612,350
37%	$510,301+	$612,351+

(Tax Brackets for 2019)

Once you have your marginal tax rate, it's important to know how much room you have before you go into the next tax bracket. For instance, if you're single and making $150,000, you can only earn $10,000 more before you jump into the next tax bracket.

It's also important to know how much higher the next tax bracket is. Keeping with the prior example (of a single person making $150,000), they are currently in the 24% marginal tax bracket. But if they start earning more than $160,725, then their marginal tax rate will jump up to 32%.

We'll get into how this can affect you and your retirement later on in this book. But for now, it's important to have a general grasp of these two terms.

Step Three To A Tax Free Retirement: Contribute to a Roth IRA (if eligible)

A Roth IRA is a really important tool to help you avoid the retirement tax bomb and create a tax free retirement.

What is a Roth IRA? The IRA part stands for Individual Retirement Account. It is, as its name implies, an investment account for retirement, that has certain tax benefits.

The Roth part means that you pay taxes on your income as you earn it. Then, you can contribute that money to a Roth IRA, where the money you put in there can grow tax free, and when you withdraw it (under qualified circumstances) you can take it out without having to pay any taxes on it.

In other words, if you use it right, you won't have to pay taxes on this money ever again (after you contribute it into the Roth account).

As of 2019, if you are under the age of fifty, you can contribute $6,000 annually to a Roth IRA.

If you are over the age of fifty, then you can actually contribute $7,000 (the IRS allows you an extra $1,000 "catch-up" contribution).

What are some additional benefits of contributing to a Roth IRA?

1: When you pass away, your inheritors won't have to pay taxes on this money.

2. Roth IRAs do not require minimum distributions. Traditional IRAs and 401Ks require you to withdraw money from your accounts each year when you reach age 70.5 (aka, RMDs). But with a Roth IRA, there are no RMDs! So you can keep that money in your account (and let it grow tax-free) if you don't need it for income.

3. This is an important one: Distributions from Roth IRAs are not counted toward provisional income. And as we just discussed, provisional income determines whether you have to pay taxes on Social Security benefits. So having more money in Roth IRAs could

lower (or eliminate) the taxes you pay on Social Security benefits.

These benefits all sound great, but there are also a few things you need to know before contributing to a Roth IRA.

They are not deal breakers, but they are just good things to be aware of, in a general sense.

- Firstly, there is no tax deduction with Roth IRAs.
- Additionally, there are income limits with them. So it's possible you may make too much money and thereby not be eligible to contribute to one. As of 2019, if you are married and file jointly, if your income exceeds $203,000, you cannot contribute to a Roth.

Given all of its benefits, having a Roth IRA as part of your retirement plan creates a lot of flexibility as well as the ability to pay much less in taxes.

Step Four To A Tax Free Retirement:
Contribute to a Roth 401(k), 403(b), 457

A 401K, 403B, and 457 are all employer sponsored retirement plans. So you can only access these plans through a job.

What many people don't know, though, is that there is a Roth option at workplace retirement plans like the 401K, 403B, or 457.

the city !

The bad news is that not every employer offers a Roth option. But the good news is that more and more companies are adding this feature, as it frankly isn't a lot more work for them to add it on.

A Roth through your employer's retirement plan functions in many ways similar to a Roth IRA. However, there are three differences that we should explore.

First, the contribution limits are much higher with these plans. In 2019, you are able to contribute up to $19,000 to one of these Roth-based plans. That's way more than the $6,000 you can put into a Roth IRA.

total 25,000

Second, the "catch-up" contribution limit is also higher. If you are over the age of 50, you can contribute an additional $6,000 per year.

Third, there is no income limitation for these types of Roth accounts. So even people who have high incomes (and can't contribute to a Roth IRA) can contribute to a Roth through their employer sponsored plans.

As I said before, though, these Roth accounts operate very similarly to Roth IRAs. The similarities include:

- There is no tax deduction when you contribute this money
- When you withdraw the money, qualified distributions are not subject to taxes
- Your inheritors won't have to pay taxes on what they receive
- These accounts also avoid provisional income classification - potentially saving you lots of money from not paying taxes on Social Security benefits.

Step Five To A Tax Free Retirement:
Make a Roth Conversion

Do you remember how I've mentioned multiple times to seek out professional expertise before you implement the educational strategies I mention in this book? That applies to all of the strategies, but especially making a Roth Conversion.

What is a Roth Conversion? It is simply taking money that is currenting in the tax-deferred bucket, and moving it to the tax-free bucket. In other words, you take money in Traditional accounts, and put it in Roth accounts.

What's the catch? I'm glad you asked.

As you've heard many times before: there's no such thing as a free lunch. And this is true with Roth Conversions as well.

When you make this switch with your money (from Traditional to Roth), the amount that you convert (moved) is considered taxable income.

In essence: with a Roth Conversion you are locking in tax rates now, so that you don't have to pay them in the future.

If you think the tax rates you are paying now are lower than what they'll be in the future (especially because of the impending tax increases), a Roth Conversion is definitely something you should consider.

Once you move this money into a Roth account, you will enjoy the same benefits as all other Roth accounts, like we've discussed in the last two steps.

There are a couple things that you should know about these conversions:
- There is no limit on the amount that you can convert to a Roth.
- Even better, there are no income limits on conversions - so even people with high incomes can make conversions.

- *You will be paying additional taxes when you make this conversion.* So you must have a plan on how to pay for those extra taxes.

Step Six To A Tax Free Retirement: Contribute To An HSA

An HSA is a Health Savings Account. You can only get access to a HSA through your medical insurance when you have a high deductible health insurance plan.

Your plan should specify if your health insurance plan is eligible for an HSA.

When you enroll in a high deductible plan that has an HSA with it, you will be allowed to contribute up to $3,500 per person, or $7,000 into that HSA.

Now what makes these HSAs so special? Because they have what I like to call a triple tax benefit.

You see, when you contribute money into an HSA, you can deduct that from your income, thus lowering your taxable income in the year you make that contribution. In other words, you don't pay taxes on that contribution.

Then, when you invest that money, it grows tax deferred, so you don't have to pay taxes on it every year.

And finally, when you withdraw that money for a qualified medical expense, distributions are tax free as well.

So you get three great tax benefits with an HSA!

But wait...there's more!

HSA distributions also avoid that pesky provisional income classification, which as we've discussed can make your Social Security benefits taxable.

HSAs Are Not For Everyone

For all their benefits, though, HSAs are not for everyone. Why? Because some people simply shouldn't be on a high deductible health insurance plan.

If you were to have some expensive health or medical emergency, these plans require you to come out of pocket and fulfill a high deductible limit before your insurance starts helping with your bills.

For instance, imagine someone who goes to the Doctor quite often, or has a recurring illness or condition (that costs a significant amount throughout the year). Having a high deductible plan probably isn't a good idea for them.

Another person who isn't a good fit for a high deductible plan is someone who doesn't have enough income (or enough in savings) to pay the whole deductible, if they ever had some kind of medical expense.

So who is a good fit for a high deducible health insurance plan (and thus an HSA)?

Someone who is healthy, doesn't have much or any ongoing medical expenses, and has a solid emergency fund of 6 months to pay for any medical deductibles if necessary.

So at this point, we've gone through the six steps to avoid the retirement tax bomb, and create a tax free retirement.

In the next chapter, I'm going to put it all together and show you how Ricky and Lucy could have implemented these strategies in their own situation.

Key Takeaways:

- There are six steps to create a tax free retirement
- One: Calculate Your Tax Buckets. You want to have the right amounts in taxable, tax deferred, and tax free buckets. You don't want all in one

bucket, as that will limit your options and likely cost you in tax savings

- Two: Know Your Provisional Income and Marginal Tax Rate
- Three: Contribute to a Roth IRA (if eligible). If your income is on the lower end, the Roth IRA is a great way to get your money in tax-free buckets.
- Four: Contribute to a Roth 401(k), 403(b), 457. If you work at an employer that has a Roth option in their retirement account, this is a great way to contribute a large amount into the tax-free bucket, without having to worry about income limitations.
- Five: Make a Roth Conversion. A Roth Conversion makes a lot of sense for some people to get money into the tax free bucket, especially if they make too much to contribute to a Roth IRA, and their employer doesn't have a Roth option in their retirement plan. But these are tricky, so please consult a professional!
- Six: Contribute To An HSA. These won't be for everyone. But if it makes sense for you, it offers a triple tax benefit that is hard to get anywhere else in the tax code.

Free Resource:
- 6 Steps To A Tax Free Retirement
- Calculating Your Tax Buckets

Get these free resources at: www.retiretaxbomb.com

Chapter Six: Putting It All Together

Now that we know the 6 steps to a tax free retirement, let's take another look at Ricky and Lucy's situation.

What could they have done better to avoid this retirement tax bomb and create a tax free retirement?

As a reminder, here is what their financial situation looks like at age 55, 10 years before when they'd like to retire.

- They have a house worth $500,000, with no mortgage
- Ricky's 401(k) has $300,000, his IRA has $200,000 and they have $100,000 saved in mutual funds (in a non-retirement account).
- They have no debt
- Their projected Social Security benefits, at age 65, is slated to be $36,000 per year
- They want to retire with $72,000 of income
- Their net worth is $1,100,000.

Now Ricky and Lucy have done well for themselves, there's no doubt about that.

But they are highly susceptible to higher (and unnecessary) taxes in the future, which would greatly diminish the kind of retirement they hope to enjoy.

What Ricky And Lucy Should Have Done

There are some smart steps that Lucy and Ricky can take to avoid the tax train, though.

First, they could both max out a Roth IRA. They can each put in $7,000 (since they get a $1,000 catch up contribution), which would result in a total of $14,000 annually.

Second, they could lower their Traditional 401(k) contributions, and instead put some (or all) of that money in a Roth 401(k).

One thing they'd have to be aware of is understanding that since they are making Roth contributions, they'd no longer be able to deduct these 401(k) contributions from their current income, which means they'd have to pay more in taxes this year.

They would also want to make sure that they don't jump into too high of a marginal tax bracket.

Third, they can convert some of their money in Ricky's Traditional IRA into a Roth IRA.

The key here is that they wouldn't do this all at once! Instead, they would do it gradually, over time.

Since Ricky and Lucy have read this book, and consulted with a financial professional, they also are aware that they need to have some cash set aside to pay the taxes on this conversion.

Because they know that a Roth Conversion isn't about avoiding taxes (not legal, don't try it). Instead, it's about locking in lower tax rates today so that you don't have to pay higher tax rates in the future.

So they use some of the money they have in mutual funds to pay those taxes.

They also are very mindful of how much they convert on an annual basis, as they don't want to push themselves into a much higher marginal tax bracket.

Fourth, because they have a solid emergency fund, and are lucky enough to enjoy good health, they sign up for a high deductible health insurance plan that has an HSA associated with it. They wisely contribute $7,000 every year, and get the triple tax benefits that come with HSAs.

Putting It All Together

After taking those steps for the 10 years before their retirement, let's now take a look at them at age 65, and see how their retirement income comes together.

Traditional 401(k): $14,000 in annual distributions

Social Security: $36,000 in yearly benefits

Roth IRA and Roth 401(k): $16,000 annual distributions

HSA: $6,000 in annual distributions (can be used to pay for Medicare and other qualified medical expenses)

Total Annual Income: $72,000

Ricky and Lucy's Tax Buckets

As you can see on the chart below, Ricky and Lucy wisely utilized all three tax buckets.

They don't have all of their money in one bucket, which would lower their flexibility and potentially cause them to pay much more in taxes.

Instead, they have practiced something us finance nerds call tax diversification.

	When Will It Be Taxed?	
Taxable Bucket	Tax-Deferred Bucket	Tax Free Bucket
$60,000	$500,000	$500,000

By doing such a good job with diversifying their tax buckets, it means that….

Ricky and Lucy's Retirement Is Now Tax-Free!!!

How in the world is this possible!?!

Let's go through their tax free income one by one.

Social Security: Their provisional income is low enough that their Social Security benefits are not taxed.

How? Because they used Roth and HSA accounts to generate income, and neither is counted as provisional income. So since they are below the provisional income threshold, none of their Social Security benefits will be taxed.

As a result, this saves them thousands of dollars per year on taxes. Over their lifetime, it will save them over a hundred thousand dollars!

Tax-Deferred Accounts: Ricky and Lucy only withdraw $14,000 from their tax-deferred accounts on an annual basis. Which is much lower than their standard deduction ($27,000 for a married couple over 65 as of 2016).

Therefore, these withdrawals aren't taxed!

What's even better about this is that they never had to pay taxes on this money.

How? Because when they were working, they deferred the taxes on it until their retirement. And now that they're in retirement, since they wisely utilized the standard deduction to offset those distributions, they owe no taxes on it now. So due to careful planning, this money was never taxed!

Tax-Free: As the name states, this money is tax free!

Ricky and Lucy can take money from this bucket (coming from Roth and HSA accounts) to help to meet their living expenses, along with their Social Security benefits and tax-deferred distributions.

And they don't have to worry about paying any taxes on this.

Further, these distributions don't count toward provisional income, which means that we don't have to worry about Social Security benefits becoming taxable.

To reiterate, here is what Ricky and Lucy have accomplished:
-No taxes come from Tax-Free accounts. *Roths*
-No taxes come from Social Security benefits.
-No taxes come from Tax-Deferred accounts.
-Ricky and Lucy are in the zero percent tax bracket (sounds nice, right?).

Key Takeaways:

- You have to make sure you use each bucket, with the right amounts, correctly!
- For the taxable bucket, there should be six to twelve months of expenses.
- For the tax deferred bucket, try to match distributions with your standard deductions so there is no taxable income. *other than pension*
- Once you get the right amounts in taxable and tax deferred buckets, any extra money should be redeployed into tax-free accounts.
- Don't do this all at once, try to make changes over the course of many years
- Be careful about bumping into a new, higher marginal tax bracket
- Act while tax rates are at historic lows! Taxes will go up on January 1, 2026 and there is good reason to believe they will go even higher after that. Don't leave a tax bomb in your retirement account!
- Always consult a financial professional before implementing these strategies

Some Parting Thoughts (And An Incredible Offer)

I want to again congratulate you for picking up this book and thinking through how to have the best retirement possible.

Taxes are an essential, and often overlooked, part of retirement.

I also hope that this book helped educate you on some of the financial challenges facing our country, as well as gave you ideas on how you can avoid being stuck in a higher tax environment.

At this point, you probably have a decent idea of what you and your family need to do. The only thing left for you to do is to actually take action.

Far too often, us humans get stuck in procrastination, knowing we should probably do something, but putting it off for whatever reason.

I can't encourage you enough to not make this mistake with your financial life.

If you would like guidance on what you should do, as well as someone to help implement everything, I have a special offer for you.

For folks who are interested in my services, I can help you create a One Page Retirement Plan that will outline everything I think you should be doing to have a comfortable, stress free retirement.

And the best part? It's completely free.

No, it won't be a sales pitch. My goal is to help you understand what you need to do to plan for your retirement, and then determine if you should implement it on your own or seek professional help.

In case you're wondering, here are some of the things I help people with:

- Tax Savings Strategies (so you pay what you owe in taxes, but you don't leave Uncle Sam a tip)
- Retirement Analysis (so you can determine when, how much income, you'll have in retirement)
- Retirement Paycheck Strategy (so you can switch from 3 decades of earned income to turning your investments into a reliable paycheck stream)
- Social Security Optimization (so you can maximize a major asset that you've worked so hard for)
- Estate Planning (so your assets go to where you want them to go, and we make sure the

people important to you make decisions for you if you are not able to do so yourself)

- Medicare Planning (so you select the best health insurance plan for you, given your health history and medical needs, affordability, travel desires, and more)
- Long Term Care Planning (so that you have a plan for if (and likely when), you need some type of help to assist you in daily life, and you are not leaving a financial strain on your spouse or kids at that time)
- Investment Analysis (so your portfolio is ready for 3+ decades of income generation, as opposed to the 3+ decades of accumulation that you are likely used to)

If you would like your own Free, One Page Retirement Plan, to go over all these issues customized to your unique situation, you can get started here:

StartMyRetirement.US

Thank you for reading, and I wish you the very best in your retirement!

Oh, I almost forgot. One last thing: If you found this book really helpful, and that the value in it exceeded the price you paid for it, would you consider making a donation so that I can continue to write to and educate as many retirees as possible?

I make all of my books free on my website (FreeRetirementBooks.com), as well as price them very affordably on Amazon. I do this because there are too many people out there who need help, and I don't want price to be an impediment from them getting closer to their retirement goals.

Your generous donation would ensure that I can continue to help as many people as possible have the best retirement possible.

You can donate here: https://bit.ly/ForthrightDonate

Get Your Free Bonus

Congrats on getting all the way through this book!

To supplement your understanding of the topics and strategies we've covered, I have created a membership website.

The site is full of resources, worksheets, and videos that will help you have the retirement you deserve. The best part? It's completely free.

You can access it at www.retiretaxbomb.com

When you sign up, here's what you'll receive:
-Video breakdown of the strategies we discuss
-Worksheets and PDFs that you can customize to your specific situation. Specifically, you will get:
> -Retirement Readiness Checklist
> -Retirement Income Worksheet
> -How To Avoid Losing $100,000 in Social
>   Security Benefits
> -8 Steps to a Worry-Free Retirement
> -Calculating Your Tax Buckets
> -6 Steps To A Tax Free Retirement

-Access to all additional resources and links

To get these helpful resources, go to
www.retiretaxbomb.com

Made in the USA
Monee, IL
08 May 2022